Hitler's New Shower

Opiates Made 'Clear'

Judah,

Truth Flasher Books

Printed in the United States of America

First Printing, 2018

ISBN: 9781720150954

Crown King, Arizona

You may correspond with the Author of this work at the following url:

JudahVisionMail@Gmail.com

Table of Contents I

Table of Contents II

The United Opiate-Scams of America

1. The American Nightmare

As we watched the SuperBowl in two thousand seventeen, the Americans who died from opiate overdose that year could've filled Aloha Stadium. And according to Doctor Sanjay Gupta, the man who declined Obama's Surgeon General Appointment, 'eighty percent of the world's pain pills are consumed in the United States but we only make up five percent of the *world* population.' I could numb your mind with the size of this monster all day long—every news show and documentary does so—but today we'll unmask some of the villains *behind* this human tragedy. *As for me*, I can quantify the problem in a sentence: For ten years I was imprisoned by opiates, to which I also lost my big brother.

And if this story were to end here, it would simply be a short, sad show with a happy ending. But what most Americans *don't* know is that it's much more than that: The so called 'Opiate Epidemic,' is an epic tale of conspiracy, murder—*genocide rather*—and greed.

My next statement didn't mean much until I'd had some time to ponder over it but, after which, it made me terribly angry: I was *painlessly* cured from the 'disease' of opiate addiction, *overnight*, in a Tijuana basement. Why? The cure to opiate addiction, in America, is *illegal!*

2. The Dilemma

In the little time I spent in Narcotics Anonymous, the first thing I learned there was: "Admitting that you have a problem is the first step to recovery." Well, in the unforgettable....paraphrased words of a great American astronaut:

> "*Houston, **we** have a problem.*"
>
> '*Jack' Swigert*

Hello, my name is 'Judah,' and *no*....I'm no longer a drug addict. But this whole fiasco made for a pretty good story so, I *am* now the author of a prose piece which documents my transition back to my non-addicted, old self. And after flying home from Mexico in 2014, I had a life-altering decision to make: Though I felt like I'd gotten away with the greatest jewel heist in the world, the truth about this so-called 'disease' began to weigh heavy on my mind and heart.

There were only two choices: I could either, a.) go home and pretend like nothing happened, which seemed to make a lot more sense, or I could, b.) tell my crazy story in a futile attempt at convincing the world that I had actually found an overnight cure to opiate addiction, just across 'the wall.' But was it really that simple? Remember, just like you, I too had been listening to the alarming size and shape of this 'incurable disease,' blaring on the evening news.

At the time of this film, I've been opiate-free for nearly 5 years; I was a chemical prisoner for ten. The modality of treatment I used was a psychedelic root bark called Ibogaine, which grows at the base of a shrub from Gabon, Africa—a right of passage for the Bwiti tribe. [cue sound effect: record scratching] You heard right the first time: Ibogaine is a psychedelic which temporarily, partially paralyzes the patient, and induces what can be up to 3 days of very realistic visions. It was the most beautiful miracle in the world.

I spent the balance of that single week getting massages, doing yoga, I had my teeth drilled with **no** anesthetic, and then just tooled around the city of "TJ" with the guys. I wasn't on a single chemical substance after a decade of reckless drug abuse! It was a hoot! No rehab. No scrubbing toilets with toothbrushes. No crying family. No cravings. No 'disease.' I was just….done. It was like a science-fiction movie but my friend it wasn't; it was all real. I used over fourteen-hundred Oxy-pills that last month alone, along with some heroin. I'm sure you will find this hard to believe but, I never tapered a milligram. In fact, while I do not suggest or condone such behavior, I went on quite the bon-voyage bender the week prior.

My daughter's best friend's older brother has been in 'rehab' for nearly a year and he's still, 'not ready.' Her girlfriend is getting dressed for school with her every morning this week because her parents are staring at him through a one-way mirror. Face-to-face contact is strictly prohibited. Her brother has a shaved head and has become a man through that chicken-wire-reenforced glass in Utah. This is the type of pressure that made me break my silence and turned my life upside-down.

There's no sense of betrayal by your country, like coming-to in a Tijuana basement, completely healed of the so-called 'disease' of addiction, after a decade of savage opiate abuse. I was once again my familiar old-self after arriving home from Tijuana (only a week later), and I had questions. This film will quantify this so-called 'disease' which has little to do with the patient, but has *everything* to do with the medical practices of this country, namely, a broken information filter at the FDA and the DEA, and the true disease which currently inflicts our Federal Government, doctors, and pharmaceutical companies: **greed***!* Unlike the forerunners to this documentary, *we* will identify the very mechanism which drives this problem, *and,* we will also unmask some of the villains who've been pulling the levers behind the curtains of this terrible manmade apocalypse.

3. Safe Painkiller 'Gone to Pot'

Around the time I flew to Mexico for treatment, the airwaves in Arizona were aglow with commercials blasting both sides of the legalization-of-recreational-marijuana-debate. Prop two hundred five wasn't even set to go on the ballot until two thousand sixteen but, there already seemed to be quite a deal more commercial interest in this measure than most. It seemed as if every commercial break was jammed with images of familiar-looking candies which contained marijuana, as babies crawled around, accompanied by a serious-sounding narrator who sternly warned Phoenicians of the ill-effects of marijuana, which had, *supposedly*, plagued the citizens of Colorado after launching their legalization measures. Namely: the commercials warned of collected tax dollars which never reached their intended institutions. I remember watching these commercials and being overcome with dread that these horrible people in Colorado hadn't used the money for what it had been earmarked for—*the children.*

But, as with most mud-slinging during election cycles, a little research revealed that this too was an out-and-out lie: The Denver Post reported in June of two thousand eighteen that the schools in Colorado had received nearly a half-Billion dollars in Marijuana-generated revenue with which to update their ailing school system. Unfortunately, just like the blind trust placed in the FDA and DEA, I, along with most Americans today, just assumed that the 'greatest country in the world' had our backs and wouldn't allow such a great lie to be broadcast throughout our land...*but I will let you be the judge of that...*

As time passed, I became fascinated with the *medical marijuana* and *opiate epidemic* debates which were both fast approaching a rapid boil; and it seemed like every evening news program served-up at least a sliver of the opiate fiasco, just as they probably will again tonight. And what began for me as the casual google-search of a person or company-name that flashed in a story or ad, had quickly began to take shape as one of the greatest conspiracies that America had *never* heard of. Remarkably, I'd begun to realize that this was more than just a 'War on Drugs,' it was a *War on Americans*. It was a *War on Truth*. *This was War on the Mind itself...*

As these anti-marijuana-commercials grew more prolific and nasty, I'd chased the financial source of these rantings to a mysterious company, in Chandler, Arizona; the name of this company is, *Insys Therapeutics.* And its billionaire founder's name, John Kapoor. To my great astonishment, Insys Therapeutics was knee-deep in the development of a prescription medical-marijuana-product they called, *Syndros*, which, as their ads boast: 'Is the first and only medically approved Dronabinol'—aka, sublingual prescription marijuana-spray, on which they had somehow gotten FDA approval to bring to market. At this point, it became infinitely clear to me, *exactly* why Insys had been meddling in our Arizona voting process. A complete marijuana reformation measure would've nullified the necessity for this product altogether in the state of Arizona, since anyone and everyone could walk into a store and buy the same product in the same or another form over-the-counter.

This was huge! Since Insys's medical marijuana breath-spray disrupted the very philosophy of the DEA which implies that, 'marijuana *has no* medical value,' one of the two criterium for marijuana's *illegal* Schedule One status. The result of which was, a new DEA Schedule Two status which would be enjoyed *only* by the drug Dronabinol, *but*, leaving marijuana, itself, in its all-natural and unmolested form, as an infamous Schedule One drug; *there was the gun*, still smoking, right in front of me.

Schedule Two drugs include powerful narcotics such as, **cocaine**, morphine and **prescription painkillers**; DEA Schedule Two narcotics are described as narcotics which simply have, 'a high probability of abuse,' implying that Schedule Two drugs such as '**painkillers**' are, '*not*, addictive.' Can you believe that? Through all of this, our Federal government still cannot even admit that this poison is 'addictive.'

This groundbreaking move wasn't only a clear violation of the DEA's own dogmatic philosophy for scheduling dangerous drugs—a process and creed which seems to be carved in stone—but, moreover, it demonstrated a strong link of collusion between the DEA and Insys; after all, let's not forget that, the whole time Insys was filing applications at the DEA and FDA, they seemed to be making headline news daily, with the most egregious charges our federal agencies could drum-up. In the end, here is what it had amounted to: this evil man spent his own money to prevent Americans from an over-the-counter, non-addictive pain reliever which could potentially improve the quality of life—and even save the lives-of—millions, only because he was knee-deep in the overwhelming expense of bringing to market a *prescription* version of a drug which could be grown unattended in your backyard. And somehow it worked!

So tell me: How *did* Insys skirt the fact that the DEA considers marijuana to be a 'highly addictive drug,' with, 'no medical value,' simply based on a patented spray delivery-system which did nothing to change the chemical compound of the drug being delivered? Wouldn't the THC delivered just be more 'dangerous' and 'addictive' than marijuana? Since it would be *more* concentrated and faster-acting than the demonized little flower that now sits at the top of a heap of the world's most dangerous drugs, according to our sick-minded DEA? These inconsistencies are alarming red flags since human lives are at stake, and should no-longer just be blindly accepted by Americans.

All-in-all, Insys had donated five hundred thousand dollars to *Arizonans for Responsible Drug Policy*, a group opposing marijuana legalization in Arizona. After which, 51.32% of Arizonans voted *Nay* to the proposition, and 48.68%, *Yea*. If you're counting, over-the-counter marijuana failed by a margin of just 2.64%. So, undoubtedly, this company, single-handedly affected the outcome of a local election, in what was ultimately a successful campaign *against* the legalization of safe and effective, all-natural painkiller: marijuana... But how did this one guy, John Kapoor, manage to accomplish the overturning of federal legislation in order to sell a drug which literally 'grows on trees?'

We will get to that but first, this raises another tired old point, but one which is worth mentioning here: Marijuana, a proven painkiller, has never been directly linked to death by overdose to a single case, yet, alcohol killed nearly ninety-thousand Americans in two thousand eighteen according to the National Institute of Health—well-over double those killed by opiates—yet, Americans will be cheerfully smashing cans on their foreheads at Super Bowl parties allover the United States this year. I'm certainly not recommending the prohibition of *alcohol*, football, or smashing cans on your forehead for that matter; but remember, the very basis on which the DEA classifies a Schedule One illegal drug is determined as one having, 'a high potential for abuse and **no medical value**,' which, seems to describe drugs like alcohol and nicotine by name. Think about it, when was the last time *you* were prescribed a, *cocktail*, or, a *cigarette?*

Simply stated: Cigarettes, a worthless drug **which currently kills around a dozen times as many people as opiates** are currently being offered *without a doctor's prescription*; barring children, anyone can simply walk in and purchase this poison to which the American government, the DEA and FDA, haven't raised an eyebrow. Does this not appear to be a textbook case of 'look at the monkey?' Invariably, I maintain that one *should* have the right to enjoy a cigarette if one chooses to do-so, so long as it doesn't compromise the rights of others.

According to the *CDC (the Center for Disease Control and Prevention)* website, ***four hundred eighty-thousand die from cigarette smoke each year in America***, 'with more than forty-one thousand of these deaths from exposure to *secondhand* smoke.' Meaning that, cigarettes aren't just 'addictive,' lacking 'medical value,' and even *deadly* to four hundred forty-thousand people per year **in America alone**, but smoking even kills *the guy sitting next to you as you do-so*. So much so, that the CDC warns that **second hand smoke, *alone*, even kills thousands more than *opiates* annually**.

In light of all of this confusion, complete 'idiocracy,' and misinformation at the highest level of education and governance, it seems that America's dreams of offering a 100% safe pain management solution have literally *gone to pot*. Which means that America will likely be left relying on 'fringe' information sources like this book from which to glean the truth about this ugly mechanism of evil; which in most cases, will be found *after* a family has been completely destroyed by this affliction.

The saying, 'gone to pot' had evolved into a common euphemism by the sixteen-hundreds, and describes those who'd fallen victim to cannibals; implying that the unfortunate soul had fallen into a cannibal's cooking cauldron and found themselves swimming amongst sliced vegetables in the warming broth of a human stew, for which you are the protein. And though the saying *doesn't* refer to *cannabis* as many think, I thought this imagery would prove quite-fitting here, as the title of this chapter.

4. Breath-Spray from Hell

Over the next several years, the laundry list of criminal activities in which Insys was involved was even enough to make Al Capone blush. I really wasn't even following the case; at this point, my life almost felt like a theater piece or a movie script. There I would be, working, and a newsflash would cause my phone to chime, I'd look down, and....Yahtzee! There on my phone, I would see a banner which read something like: '*Billionaire Charged With Bribing Doctors to Prescribe Opioids,*' or, '*Opioid Billionaire's Indictment Opens New Window on Epidemic.*'

But, much to my horror, no media outlet ever so much as cracked the shades to these amazing 'windows' into this 'epidemic.' And it also seemed that the mastermind of this great charade, *John Kapoor,* was still somehow being *insulated* from the law. It quickly became clear to me that this story would *not* unfold through our provided default media channels, so, by this time *I'd* actually taken possession of the story, and began some gumshoe work myself. And the events that unfolded from here are nothing if not mind-bending...

It was on October twenty-six, two thousand seventeen, when I discovered that along with their medical marijuana 'breath-spray,' Insys was also dealing a highly deadly **opiate breath-spray!** *The Motley Fool* reported the following, under the headline, 'The Double Whammy That Sent Marijuana Stock Insys Therapeutics Crashing as Much as 30%':

Today, Wall Street found out that the billionaire founder of Insys Therapeutics, John Kapoor, who still owns a majority stake in the company and was CEO as recently as January two thousand seventeen, was arrested. He's been charged with engaging in conspiracies to commit racketeering, mail fraud, and wire fraud, based on the federal indictment filed in a Boston court. The charges, which Kapoor's attorney has denied, suggest that Kapoor and a handful of other executives devised a scheme to pay speaker fees and bribes to medical practitioners in return for prescribing **Subsys** to non-cancer patients. This was also a means to defraud insurers, according to the documents filed in Boston.

Subsys, the drug described in the article mentioned, is yet another drug product under the corporate umbrella of Insys: *Subsys*, is an **opiate**-based, sublingual, *painkiller*-spray... A mist-delivery-system which is sprayed under the tongue, just like the marijuana product on which, *Insys*—the very same company—had hedged their bets, when they financed ads targeting the anti-legalization campaign in Arizona, to thwart the bill which would allow for legal over-the-counter marijuana.

So, as with any Hegelian strategy of controlled conflict, it seems that *Insys* too was betting on both sides of this frenzied debate. And though the article mentions a laundry list of charges against Kapoor, one charge they forgot to bring forth or were conveniently ignorant-to, was, *murder! Serial murder!*

As early as two thousand fifteen, multiple news sources were reporting that hundreds of patients had died due to the product's 'fast acting' pain relief 'delivery system.' And doctors associated with the company were being hauled-off in handcuffs due to the extraordinary explosion in overdose among their patients. And though the damage caused by this company for profit, in terms of loss of human life, isn't so easily quantified, what we do know is that, at least 'hundreds' *have* been killed by Insys, using their handy, new, patented, fast-acting delivery system for one of the most powerful **opiates** ever synthesized. If you're interested in a course for your own research, the criminal activities in which this company was partaking, in multiple states across this nation, are *staggering*.

I don't wanna get off-track here but, it's worth noting that Insys probably wasn't terribly worried about all the bad press concerning dead human beings, since, Insys had already had the forethought to formulate a so-called 'cure' for their new disease *Subsys*—their overdose-causing Fentanyl spray...Remarkably, Insys was simultaneously developing a patented, oral spray, anti-overdose-version of what I like to refer to as the 'Pulp-Fiction-overdose-kit,' a buccal version of Naloxone, a drug which is normally administered to reverse overdose.

So, at the same time, *Insys*, was developing Syndros which was being touted as a THC-based safe alternative to opioid painkillers, Subsys which was being billed as the 'breakthrough' cure for cancer pain—which was also killing patients by the bus-load—and, a Naloxone spray to bring you back from overdose, just in case you took too much Subsys...So, in plainer words, this same company was producing the 'disease,' the 'cure,' and a safe alternative pain reliever, just in case the patient survived the 'disease' and the 'cure' but still needed to treat pain in a natural and responsible manner.

What most sources didn't mention about these Fentanyl deaths, however, is that fentanyl had been killing opiate addicts for decades. In fact, Fentanyl, according to the infinite sources on the internet, is somewhere between 'fifty' and 'ten thousand times stronger than morphine,' depending on where you look...Which, I know sounds ridiculous, especially since many of these sources are considered to be very reputable. For example: The CDC injury center cites that Fentanyl is 'fifty to 100 times stronger than morphine,' while the *DEA* database has *Fentanyl* locked-in at 'fifty times stronger than morphine.'

In around two thousand sixteen, the DEA even stated that a new Fentanyl cocktail which was surfacing in the illicit opiate market was testing at 'ten thousand times stronger than morphine' and was being referred to as the 'gray death.' But even if Fentanyl is only twice as strong as morphine, I would propose that this chemical *shouldn't* be packaged in a *rapid* delivery system as Insys had done.

Keep in mind, too, that, this pharmaceutical 'breakthrough'—*Fentanyl* in an *oral spray*—came at a time when this so-called 'gray death' was hovering through cities across the nation. One could scarcely watch the evening news without these heroic batches of 'gray-death'-Fentanyl being mentioned, and waves of Americans have been swept away in this whirlwind since. Due to the impeccable timing of the arrival of this chemical death sentence, it almost appears as if some hidden hand were secretly herding this licit market into the open mouth of gray death.

Fentanyl is predictably deadly! So tell me...How *did* the DEA *and* FDA overlook Subsys's deadly little stumbling block which should certainly have prevented Insys from providing Fentanyl in a rapid delivery system? Again, the answer is, *greed!*

You may cynically be whispering to yourself, *well*... 'despite Mr. Kapoors actions, he is merely one bad actor and that proves absolutely nothing.' In response to which, I would like to introduce to you the *Sackler Brothers, Purdue Pharma, and the OxyContin Dynasty of Opiates—the financial and legal trailblazers for our current opiate plague.*

5. Paging Doctor WHO?

In the mid-nineties, OxyContin, the opium which led *me* down the rabbit hole, was being touted as the next 'non-addictive,' miracle cure for pain and addiction. And as it turns out, Insys was using a tactic pulled right from the pages of OxyContin maker, *Purdue Pharma's* timeworn playbook, when *they* traded profit for, cold, gray, dead human beings with dried, crusted foam trailing from the corners of their mouths.

Decades before Insys, Purdue released a paper undermining this most-powerful drug's addictive nature. Again, *just as did Insys*, Purdue then hired an army of doctors, government scum, and ill-informed drug-peddlers, who wined, dined, and paid the doctors to spread the lies which kicked off the OxyContin wave of so-called 'non-addictive' opiates.

We've all heard of OxyContin, but what exactly is this legendary poison? And what makes its patent so special? Well....The only active ingredient contained in OxyContin's miracle medication, is, *Oxycodone*—the same opium which had been in Percocet for decades. Your doctor and the crooks at the FDA & DEA somehow missed the only active controlled substance in both of these drugs, when awarding Purdue with this patent.

Then what makes Oxy so special if OxyContin and Percocet are merely the exact same chemical? *Here's the one, dirty little secret which has caused all the fuss*: Percocet comes in five to ten milligram tablets but OxyContin is available in twenty, to eighty milligram tablets. Which means that the FDA and DEA both rubber-stamped OxyContin's patent even though it was just a cleaner version of Percocet, which was simply being offered in a package eight to sixteen times *stronger* than Percocet. I'm calling it, *'Atomic Percocet!'* Now you know why OxyContin was so popular! *Pow!*

OxyContin's new patented 'ER packaging' allowed Purdue, **only**, to provide its customers with sixteen-times the amount of the exact same active ingredient in Percocet: Oxycodone! That's right, OxyContin was just a giant Percocet after the addict easily removed this candy's outer wrapper! Purdue patented its 'time release packaging' for the poison. Purdue then implied that this 'packaging' made the drug 'non-addictive.' After which, Washington's crooked politicians and their evil servants at the FDA and DEA rubber-stamped the paperwork...and, just like that, Hitler's shiny new shower was plumbed and tiled. Purdue cornered the opium market, and single-handedly quadrupled the opium consumption in the United States. As a consequence to their corruption and greed, Purdue also quadrupled the mortality rate for these evil drugs. How did this one get past, everyone?

On may third, two thousand seventeen, a dozen members of Congress sent a letter to the World Health Organization, warning it of the deceptive practices Purdue Pharma was planning to unleash on the rest of the world through a new global dope-spreading campaign under the new corporate veil, Mundipharma:

Dear Dr. Chan:

We write to warn the international community of the deceptive and dangerous practices of Mundipharma International—an arm of Purdue Pharmaceuticals. The greed and recklessness of one company and its partners helped spark a public health crisis in the United States that will take generations to fully repair. We urge the World Health Organization (WHO) to do everything in its power to avoid allowing the same people to begin a worldwide opioid epidemic. Please learn from our experience and do not allow Mundipharma to carry on Purdue's deadly legacy on a global stage.

Mundipharma International is a network of pharmaceutical companies owned by the Sackler Family. The Sacklers also own and operate Purdue Pharmaceuticals, the privately held company that developed and marketed OxyContin. Internal documents revealed in court proceedings now tell us that since the early development of OxyContin, Purdue was aware of the high risk of addiction it carried. Combined with the misleading and aggressive marketing of the drug by its partner, Abbott Laboratories, Purdue began the opioid crisis that has devastated American communities since the end of the nineteen nineties. Today, Mundipharma is using many of the same deceptive and reckless practices to sell OxyContin abroad.

OxyContin was approved by the US Food and Drug Administration (FDA) in nineteen ninety-five. Though executives at Purdue were aware that their dosing recommendations were ineffective for many patients, and that the formulation and dosing raised the risk of addiction, they advertised OxyContin as a solution for day-to-day pain. Purdue and its marketing partner Abbott used gifts and free meals to develop relationships with physicians, who would then prescribe the painkiller to patients with ordinary pains, rather than the severe, long-term pain associated with end-stage cancer [which is precisely what Insys did]. Purdue's efforts were effective:

at their height, OxyContin sales reached three Billion a year.

Meanwhile, cases of opioid-related substance use disorder skyrocketed. By two thousand nine, emergency room visits related to prescription drugs reached one point two million cases, with opioid pain relievers, and especially OxyContin, being the most prominent cause for visits and fatalities. People were dying.

Moreover, as the rate of prescription opioid use and related overdoses rose, increased demand spilled into the illicit drug trade. The enormous market for opioids created in the wake of the OxyContin boom, combined with the much lower cost of heroin compared with prescription medications, meant an explosion in heroin use and dramatic increase in the rate of overdoses. As many as eighty percent of heroin users started out using prescription opioids.

Today, in spite of intensive efforts to address this crisis, the rate of overdose deaths continues to rise. In two thousand fifteen alone, more than thirty-three thousand people died as a result of opioid overdoses in the United States.

A major piece of the current US strategy to address the opioid epidemic is to provide physicians and patients with information about the risks associated with opioids, as well as effective alternatives for pain management. With collaboration between prescribers and lawmaker, prescriptions for OxyContin in the US have dropped nearly forty percent since two thousand ten...

Okay, wait a minute...these guys and gals might be giving themselves a *little* too much credit in this last paragraph. 'Prescriptions for OxyContin in the US' may have 'dropped,' but fatalities by opiate overdose continued to rise, dramatically, since what these fellas *failed* to mention is that, OxyContin changed their 'packaging' in 'two thousand ten' when OxyContin sales 'dropped forty percent,' as mentioned. Purdue's *new* recipe caused the pill to turn to slime when mixed with a solvent in preparation to inject or insufflate, which clogged addicts needles and noses; this 'forty percent' decline in Oxy use, was merely due to the fact that Oxy could no-longer be *abused* when used intravenously and sniffed. And if these Congressmen would've just conducted a cursory internet search, they would've realized that generic oxycodone and heroin use had skyrocketed in the absence of the old 'packaging' of OxyContin, which is precisely why the death toll for opiates continued to rise after their so-called information-spreading 'strategy.'

But then again, we *know* that these Congressmen and women were already aware of this fact, because two paragraphs earlier they clearly stated: 'The enormous market for opioids created in the wake of the OxyContin boom, combined with the much lower cost of heroin compared with prescription medications, meant an explosion in heroin use and dramatic increase in the rate of overdoses.' These twelve just overlooked the slight tweak that OxyContin had made to their 'packaging' formula in two thousand ten or they would've seen that this was exactly what had caused them to naively believe that it was *their* so-called information-spreading strategy which had caused

OxyContin sales to drop that forty percent, when in fact, addicts just no-longer cared for the 'packaging' in which this poison was locked. The sad takeaway from this fatal oversight is, these men and women of Congress falsely believe that our current treatment for this crisis is somehow adequate, when it clearly continues to kill Americans by the stadium-load.

Twelve Congressmen Letter continued…

…In response to the growing scrutiny and diminished U.S. sales, the Sacklers have simply moved on. On December eighteen, the Los Angeles Times published an extremely troubling report detailing how in spite of the scores of lawsuits against Purdue for its role in the U.S. opioid crisis, and tens of thousands of overdose deaths, Mundipharma now aggressively markets OxyContin internationally. In fact, Mundipharma uses many of the same tactics that caused the opioid epidemic to flourish in the US, though now in countries with far fewer resources to devote to the fallout.

In some places, Mundipharma companies hold 'training seminars,' where doctors are encouraged to overlook their concerns about opioids and prescribed painkillers for chronic pain. Some Mundipharma materials have attempted to downplay the risk of addiction, recalling Purdue's early OxyContin marketing in the nineteen nineties. Those marketing materials eventually led to federal drug misbranding charges and a six hundred thirty-five million dollar judgment against Purdue. Mundipharma also brings American doctors to other countries to promote the use of opioid painkillers to local physicians. This too, was a common practice by Purdue to push OxyContin in the US.

The International health community has a rare opportunity to see the future. Though the rate of opioid use disorder remains relatively low outside of the United States, that can change rapidly. The rate is likely to rise if events follow the same pattern as in the United States, starting with the irresponsible—and potentially criminal— marketing of prescription opioids. From nineteen ninety-nine to two thousand fourteen, the rate of opioid-related overdose deaths in the United States nearly quadrupled. Opioid use disorder is on the rise globally now—current European rates are similar to rates in the United States in the early two-thousands, and the WHO has struggled to address rising dependence on Tramadol in at least eight countries.

We urge the WHO to learn from our experience and rein in this reckless and dangerous behavior while there is still time.

Do not allow Purdue to walk way from the tragedy they have inflicted on countless American families simply find new markets and new victims elsewhere.

A court document filed in a US Court in Washington State on behalf of a community who'd been financially, mentally, and physically lain waste by the 'fallout' of 'Atomic Percocet,' included this letter from twelve concerned congressmen. The document filed in the courts adds the following to this letter:

Purdue's pivot to untapped markets, after extracting substantial profits from communities like Thurston County and leaving the County to address the resulting damage, underscores that its actions have been knowing, intentional, and motivated by profits throughout this entire tragic story.

Just to summarize here: An Act of Congress in the nineties paved the way for long-term 'pain management' in the United States, at the behest of a privileged family who was awarded a new patent for a painkiller which was merely a sixteen-times stronger version of Percocet, which passed the scrutiny of the DEA and FDA—who should be our greatest minds in a field in which they are paid to protect Americans—and this 'Atomic Percocet' went-on to snuff the lives of who-knows-how-many human beings. Twelve Congressmen then went through the trouble of writing this harsh letter to the World Health Organization, warning of an ongoing genocide in the United States—as if they were desperately appealing to the grace of a comic superhero— because they feared it would consume the rest of the world. And you mean to tell me that if all of these checkpoints would've just been paying attention, they all would've realized that OxyContin simply amounted to a handful of ordinary Percocet? Meanwhile, where are these 'twelve Congressmen' now?

Shouldn't these twelve congressmen be standing on boxes in the streets, screaming from megaphones right now? But, moreover, where are the other four hundred twenty-three Congressmen who simply went-on about their lives? And, perhaps most-disturbing, why aren't our news channels blaring the words of this letter from every TV and radio? And why aren't they firmly emblazoned on the front pages of every newspaper? But instead, sadly, it for some reason takes great skill just to find a copy of this warning letter on the internet. Why? Again, invariably, the answer is Greed!

It appears that, not only has the entire world ignored this 'rare opportunity to see the future,' issued by these twelve Congress-people, but the citizens of our own country have scarcely heard a whisper about these terrible warnings, leaving people like John Kapoor of Insys Therapeutics to continue slaughtering Americans for profit, using the very same organized criminal tactics which Purdue Pharma had originally used to peddle OxyContin.

It's very disturbing to see that this tiny slice of Congress showed enough goodwill to forewarn the rest of the world about this genocide but somehow lost their voices here in America. But, I would still like to give these twelve Congressmen an honorable mention just for sticking their necks out enough to feel the cold, razor sharp blade of commerce graze their throats. Here is a comprehensive list of the good guys (and gals) in Congress who had somehow lost their voices after sending what amounted to nothing more than a message in a bottle to warn the rest of the world: Katherine Clark, Hal Rogers, Theodore Deutch, Raúl M. Grijalva, Marcy Kaptur, William R. Keating, Ann McLane Kuster, Stephen F. Lynch, James P. McGovern, Tim Ryan, Carol Shea-Porter, and Paul D. Tonko. That's all.

I would like to remind you that there were another four hundred twenty-three men and women in Congress, who *all* should've signed this letter and then sounded the warning alarms throughout America and the world, after which, they quickly should have aided in the institution of change throughout those governments and medical care systems.

As aforementioned, the Twelve Congressmen Warning Letter stated, 'In response to the growing scrutiny and diminished US sales, the Sacklers have simply moved on.' Which really isn't a completely accurate statement either....In reality, they did something which better-resembled riding off into the sunset. On July 1, two-thousand-fifteen, Forbes.com posted an article titled: 'The OxyContin Clan: The Fourteen Billion Dollar Newcomer to Forbes two thousand fifteen List of Richest US Families.' This is how the article begins:

The richest newcomer to Forbes 2015 list of America's Richest Families comes in at a stunning Fourteen-Billion dollars. The Sackler family that owns Connecticut-based Purdue Pharma flew under the radar when **Forbes** launched its initial list of wealthiest families in July 2014, but this year they crack the top-20, edging out storied families like the Busches, Mellons and Rockefellers. How did the Sacklers build the 16th-largest fortune in the country? The short answer: making the most popular and controversial opioid of the twenty-first century—*OxyContin*.

This article, posted on **Forbes**.com, *could* be viewed as a literary 'wink' from the Forbes family to the Sackler family for *their* astounding achievements in the dope trade, since, the **Forbes** bunch too were a 'storied family' of dope dealers who can be linked back to Yale University's Order of Skull and Bones and the infamous Russell and Company. In light of the Forbes's historic participation in the Order of Skull and Bones, war, Yale, and dope-dealing, I favored news-sources from their channels for this work ;)

Here again, call me a 'conspiracy buff.' But in light of the fact that Robert Bennet **Forbes was the head of Russell and Company and his brother John Murray Forbes was a director for these Civil War era dope-dealers**, I think we may have found another 'smoking gun' linking the opium problems in America to the Order of Skull and Bones on Yale University. Coincidentally, Purdue Pharmaceuticals, the makers of OxyContin are only an hour drive from Yale

University, home of a secret society known as *the Order of Skull and Bones. Chapter 7*, titled, *Opium - Dynasty One*, will expand on this damnatory connection.

You may have heard of the infamous 'Merchants of Death' from mainstream news sources when, John **Forbes** Kerry, **initiated into the Order of Skull and Bones in nineteen sixty-six, and his cousin George Walker Bush, who entered the 'Merchants of Death' in *sixty-seven*,** faced-off for the Presidential election in a brazen Hegelian maneuver of controlled conflict. This strategy ensured that a 'Bonesman' would Preside over a term which produced the tragic events of 9/11.

The United Opiate-Scams of America

6. Advertisers of Evil

If it's not already, this is the part where I make your stomach churn: Arthur Sackler, founder of OxyContin maker Purdue Pharma, was literally inducted into the **M**edical **A**dvertising **H**all of **F**ame, by which a citation praised Arthur Sackler's achievement of, 'bringing the full power of advertising and promotion to pharmaceutical marketing.' *Yes!* Unfortunately there is such a thing as the Medical Advertising Hall of Fame. To see this mess for yourself, visit MAHF.com, scroll all the way down to the last fella on the list and click on his name, to verify Art's amazing contribution to this high-tech shell game. I also encourage you to read some of this group's ambitious reading materials. And yes, Arthur Sackler is more-or-less a god to these people.

But Art *didn't* make his way into the Medical Advertising Hall of Fame with OxyContin as you probably now suspect; he actually became the first person to pass one hundred-million dollars from the sale of a single drug: Valium. As a result of his overwhelming commercial success with combining advertising and pharmaceuticals, many chemical companies quickly followed his lead.

Arthur began his career in psychiatry but soon entered the field of medical advertising. From here, Art quickly forged a working relationship with William Menninger, who headed the Army's budding branch of Psychiatry. Menninger was outlining a treatment for 'Shell Shock' at the time which, of course, included the copious use of barbiturates as part of the treatment protocol. Sackler's new buddy's notorious playbook, *Medical 203*, became the basis of *DSM 1*—the original Diagnostic and Statistical Manual for Mental Disorders—which sounded the gun, kicking off the bonanza known now as the 'pharmacologic treatment of mental illness.' To shed some light on the spirit of this handbook from hell, the DSM even listed *homosexuality* as a 'disorder' until nineteen seventy-three.

Arthur Sackler crossed this major milestone for television drug-peddlers, pain management clinics, garden-variety wrongdoers of any sort, and crooked Politicians and PCP's, everywhere. The result of which are television ad campaigns that capture Billions from the citizens of this country today! These drug-pushing slow-motion TV ads are illegal in every country but America, and New Zealand where it *wasn't* legal until nineteen eighty-one.

After years of legal discourse, the Sackler Brothers' precious Purdue Pharma was found guilty of this American Chemical Genocide. Purdue was only court-ordered to pay six hundred-million in fines, four hundred seventy-million of which went back to the crooked American agencies who helped enable their success. This was but a tranche of the blood-money generated by their evil scam which catapulted this family into the Forbes Top Twenty Riches Families in 2015; none of which went back to the families who have been (and are still) being devastated by their manmade American plague. The payoff money reached its intended accomplice, and Purdue Pharma still offers the same-exact poison today in a slightly different 'packaging.'

It is important to remember the OxyContin story and the brutal, organized criminal tactics Purdue Pharma used to corrupt the entire American medical system—and that our government did nothing to foresee and stop this most-basic grift—since, this is the very foundation on which every subsequent wave of 'miracle' opiates will follow. Purdue set the legal stage for the chaos and death we are seeing now. Once again, it literally took the Sacklers an *Act of Congress* to change the legislation which stood in the way of this landslide of human misery which, as we speak, is now snowballing to include the rest of the world.

The first takeaway I would like the viewer to glean from this presentation is that, the ruthless organized criminal activity and basic lack of concern for human life in all of these cases is clearly evident. The motivation behind this scourge seems, to a great degree, to be the wholesale wielding of misery, destruction, and death as much as it is a massive dragnet accumulation of wealth.

The second viewer takeaway which I hope to now share with you is, the following basic idea: I think that most of us simply assume that chemical-engineering-geniuses are formulating new synthetic painkillers from scratch in a lab, behind the scenes at these pharmaceutical companies, which surely isn't the case. In all of the horrific cases we've studied thus far, these manufacturers were merely awarded a patent for the 'packaging' surrounding this poison, but that, the active ingredients inside these medicines virtually went chemically unchanged. In all cases, they were merely massive doses of the same opiate painkilling agents which had already been taking lives for decades if not centuries.

Production of *all* opioids requires a basic derivative of organic opium straw called, thebaine; also known as codeine methyl enol ether, which is an opiate alkaloid. Meaning that, in the end, just like heroin and marijuana, all painkillers are just *grown* and harvested from plants. Sixty-six percent of the world's opium straw is grown in the poppy fields of Afghanistan, most of which are being guarded by American soldiers (Youtube-search title: 'Marines grow opium for their masters' to see US Marines guarding these fields). This means that the world's prescription painkiller supply is being grown side-by-side with the plants which will produce the world's illicit opium supply of heroin. *Legal* dope is simply repackaged chemically and physically, which is where the so-called 'intellectual property'—or, 'patent'—lies. In plainer words, these painkiller 'patents' are merely a distribution of golden tickets which are awarded to these soulless families to peddle dope.

7. Opium - Dynasty One

I'll make things easy…Just in case you didn't already know: All opiates, or 'opioids,' make up the painkiller family, which are all just synthesized versions of the natural toxin, opium. Yes, the opium which is derived from the opium poppy flower—it's that simple. OxyContin, Oxycodone, Opana, Percocet, Percodan, Hydrocodone, Vicodin, Dilaudid, Codeine, Morphine, Methadone, Suboxone, Subutex, Tramadol, Hydromorphone, Darvocet, Lortab, Fentanyl, Buprenorphine, Desomorphine, Russian Krokodil, and all of the other poisons that we can barely pronounce…are all the same thing: opium.

The engineers of the American Civil War simultaneously *foresaw* the opportunity to inject the 'disease' of opiate addiction into the American culture; this is the very moment at which chains and shackles gave way to chemical bondage in America. The demand for which produced the *Opium Wars* on the other side of the world. The British East India Company—owned by an oligarchy of British Royals—then waged war in Eastern Asia in order to subdue the Eastern opium market through strategic operations in India and China. The economics of this plague produced the Opium Lords of yesteryear who forced this disease upon the entire world with America being ground zero for this disaster.

President Franklin Delano Roosevelt's grandfather, Warren Delano, made his grandson 'FDR' filthy rich with the proceeds of his Opium Dynasty while working for a company called, 'Russell and Company.' Russell and Company's founder, *Samuel Russell*, was a descendent of *Nodiah Russell* who founded Yale University. Russell and Company was awarded the golden ticket for legal dope-pedaling during the ugliest days on this soil—*the American Civil War*.

It was then by no accident that it was *Russell and Company* connected President, *Franklin Delano Roosevelt,* who helped, criminalize, regulate, and ensure that his family bloodline would profit handsomely from the distribution and use of chemical substances by Americans which has resulted in the social disaster in America today.

Roosevelt backed the *Uniform State Narcotic Act*, an unconstitutional measure which began the prohibition and demonization of marijuana in particular, which pushed unwitting Americans into his privileged Bloodline's deadly dope racket in exchange for safe escape from physical and emotional pain. This 'racket' has its English-bloodline-roots firmly planted as East India Company Directors who are all related to every single American President, *and every single Skull and Bones member*...yes, *even Obama*, Trump, *and* Hillary are all cousins! This is the *true* purpose of 'Party Vetting.' If you get a chance, you should YouTube search the following keywords: *All Presidents are Related By Blood - Including Most World Leaders!*

The Sacred Scroll of Seven Seals Series examines high-level Skull and Bones posts held within the *Congress of the Confederate States* who, after a couple of well-timed terrorist attacks forced a Civil War which no one on either side had wanted; and though their bloodline and cause *were noble*, their intentions and business plan for this war *were not*. It is profound to think that Bonesmen held so may high-level posts when you realize that there were only fifteen *Bonesmen* 'tapped' per year.

Further justifying our suspicion of this crowd, *Samuel Russell's cousin*, Samuel Huntington Russell *founded* this infamous Yale secret society, 'The Order of Skull and Bones,' on Yale University. Remarkably, on May thirty, eighteen seventy-nine, *Society Kappa Psi* which later became *Kappa Psi Pharmaceutical Fraternity* was *also* founded on the campus of *Yale University*, at an institution known then as, *Russell Military Academy*. *Russell Military Academy* was a Civil War training camp that was started by the very same founder of The Order of Skull and Bones, *William Huntington Russell; again*, on what is now the campus of Yale University.

In the year eighteen forty, Russell Military Academy—*which trained an astounding number of key men on the Union side for the Civil War*—somehow '*foresaw*' the *coming* of the American Civil War **two decades** *before the conflict began.* In light of the fact that the very same campus also spawned America's first pharmaceutical fraternity, it appears that Russell 'somehow foresaw' the massive opportunity for creating this horrible opiate plague in the process, by which a stranglehold could be kept on the industry from the shadows henceforth.

Huh, think about that…Russell's school of Civil War and a fraternity of practitioners who would manage the regulation and distribution of pain-deadening narcotics after the war were both started on the very same dirt, *at nearly the very same time.* And not a better match has been made since the hand met the glove.

According to their website, the fraternity which was founded on what is now the campus of Yale University by William Huntington Russell (the founder of The Order of Skull and Bones), the group is now:

'The oldest and largest professional pharmacy fraternity in the world, Kappa Psi was founded on May thirty, eighteen seventy-nine, in New Haven, Connecticut, and currently there are 191 chapters (111 Collegiate and 80 Graduate chapters), more than six thousand collegiate members, and over eighty-seven thousand graduate members across the United States, Canada, and the Bahamas.' The objectives of Kappa Psi include:

- To conduct a professional fraternal organization for the mutual benefit of its members;
- To develop industry, sobriety, and fellowship;
- To foster high ideals, scholarship, and pharmaceutical research;
- To support all projects which will advance the profession of pharmacy and to actively participate in them;
- To inspire in its members a deep and lasting pride in their Fraternity and in the profession of pharmacy;
- To render such other services to its members and its profession feasible and in accordance with the constitution and bylaws of the Fraternity.

Clearly I don't believe that all of these pharmaceutical tenderlings are part of an evil plot to dispatch Americans and then the rest of the world. But it's not important that newcomers to the profession be participant in the nefarious beliefs of their fraternity's forefathers and any current bad actors. So long as new initiates are offered a steady stream of misinformation from the teats from which these babes are nursed, they make far-better soldiers of evil since they truly believe in their cause and maintain the conditions in which these creeps thrive. This leaves people like Arthur Sackler and John Kapoor free to rape, pillage, and murder for hire, with academia and government agencies as unknowing dupe shills for this grift.

If we had to point fingers at the source from which this bad information flows, they'd all wag toward Yale University, who seems to be the Magna Mater of this filthy nursery. At the very least, here—at the risk of being deemed a 'conspiracy buff'—i'm afraid that, fraternity, enterprise, and marketing, have handily outpaced research, development, and medical breakthroughs.

But if we're telling the whole-truth, *Yale,* along with the rest of the Ivy League Schools, were *all* founded by the descendants of the sinister British East India Company who waged wars and enslaved indigenous peoples to grow opium which sparked an epic series of famine, which in turn killed an estimated hundred-million or more Eastern Indians in the process; East India Company was *also* responsible for the lion's share of African slaves who were brought to America, and the rest of the world.

East-India-Company-grown opium was then spread around the world to *chemically* enslave other indigenous peoples, in order to manipulate world politics and markets. It could even be argued that FDR's presidency itself is produce of this early American Opium Dynasty. I like to refer to this first American wave of opiate addiction as, 'The Great American Opium Dynasty,' which is where the opiate circus all began.

Today, the *Samuel Wadsworth Russell House* (its original owner being Samuel Russell, owner of the opium clearing house, *Russell and Company*) sits right down the road from

'The Tomb'—the infamous Temple and meeting place for the Order of Skull and Bones—on Yale's *High Street*. And, though he is memorialized and nearly worshipped there, *Sammy didn't even attend University at Yale.*

As hard as it is to separate this work from Yale and the Order of Skull and Bones, there was no avoiding their sinister campus. Americans have been brilliantly trained to stuff their fingers in their ears and begin howling *Yankee Doodle* at the top of their voice at the moment Skull and Bones is mentioned. Even though every fact and figure adds up to the decimal, to utter the words 'Skull and Bones' instantly makes you a 'kook,' or a 'conspiracy buff,' which by the efforts of these initiates has, 'lit a fire in the minds of men' which has now grown into a raging inferno.

Some have even turned up cold, bloated and blue, as was the case with journalist Tim Russert, who, after asking both John Kerry and George Bush about their grimy fraternity during their election cycle, found himself in such a state. So it is not surprising that we've all, *almost magically*, been frozen in an eternal state of dementia as our children are devoured and our land, revenue, and very thoughts, have been cleverly commandeered by this bloodline of pirates.

But to truly understand this plague and the spirit of those who've historically baited and set the traps for this financial boon, it is impossible to completely ignore these subversive bloodlines. If you care to delve into this avenue of discovery, read the *Sacred Scroll of Seven Seals Series*, by 'Judah.'

In the mid-eighteen-hundreds when these institutions were formed there was no FDA or DEA to supposedly 'educate' and police American drug use, there was no Kappa Psi Pharmaceutical Fraternity. There were no drug prohibition laws whatsoever because one was free to do as one pleased… And, shockingly, **there was also no opiate crisis in America!** *Disturbingly, it is literally the snake oil and 'patent medicine' salesman of yesteryear who are still dealing today's sanctioned dope, they are just dressed in different suits.*

Nixon, a man who was groomed by *Prescott Bush*—who surely would've been President in Nixon's place had he not lost assets to the *Trading with the Enemy Act for financing Hitler*—declared a War on Americans which he deceptively named the 'War on Drugs.' Nixon is who famously declared drug abuse, 'public enemy number one.' This was further exacerbated by the *Reagans* who reinvigorated the battle: *Nancy*, by ramping-up rhetoric and propaganda, and '*Ronnie*' who signed-off on a measure to reverse legislation which had formerly prohibited marketing by pharmaceutical manufacturers. Which, as you will learn is quite deadly.

It was on Ronald Reagan's watch that the CIA was convicted of dealing illicit cocaine in America—fueling the crack cocaine epidemic in urban America—to fund the provision of illegal weapons to Iran during the Iran Contra scandal, just as Prescott had helped to arm Hitler in World War Two. And all the while George Bush one, Prescott Bush's *son*, was Ronnie's Vice President. Bush Senior formerly served as *Director* of the CIA which was created nearly in toto by Skull and Bones members. America then quickly dismissed all of these grievous crimes against humanity and elected George W, Bush into office. And we all know how that turned out for us.

Only eleven officials were convicted for these crimes, mostly for destruction of evidence, but they too were pardoned, most by George Herbert Walker Bush on Christmas Eve, in nineteen ninety-two, just after he'd lost the White House to Bill Clinton. Which means that Ollie's sinister actions were all forgiven in a Presidential Pardon which was granted by the mastermind of this mess, *George Bush Senior*.

Oliver North's infamous trial blared for months from every news source on this planet, in which he was criminally charged for dealing cocaine in America to fund international skullduggery. Despite this fact, Oliver North went on to serve as a political contributor for CNN; Wikipedia lists Ollie as 'an American political commentator, television host, military historian, and author'—an amazing platform from which to further spin lies for this cabal, for a *convicted liar* who should've been convicted of *mass murder and high treason*.

8. Morphine - Opium Dynasty Two

Opium use had grown out of control due to the actions of Roosevelt's privileged East-India-Company-bloodline, so old-school-Pharma introduced Morphine as the 'non-addictive' cure to the opium epidemic. The discovery of morphine, named for the Greek god of dreams, was considered to be a medical wonder. By the mid eighteen-fifties, Russell and Company morphine was available in the US, just in time for the Civil War. And, once again, a victorious medical community declared that opium had been 'tamed.'

By the way, this is also when the medical industry passed a 'sharp' to the addict, as this ground-breaking new invention was all-the-rage in the medical market; but it was originally designed with a more-nefarious purpose in mind: Also known as the hypodermic needle, this vial of misery was specifically designed and patented as the cure for opium addiction. Along with the syringe, the all-new 'miracle drug,' *'Morphia'* was being sent home with opium-addicted patients for outpatient based 'treatment.' And being in the dark, early evening shadows of the American Civil War, patients came by the rabbles. With maladies ranging from the common cold to shredded and lost limbs, Morphine was being passed out like breath mints and an astounding four hundred-thousand Americans became hopelessly addicted in the process.

Morphine, was the spark of chemical inspiration which initially caused this whole laboratory-hatched American 'disease.'

9. Heroin - Opium Dynasty Three

Gather 'round, ladies and gentleman...and step right up! I give you: the all-new 'Miracle Anti-Addiction Drug—Heroin.' The miracle answer to addiction has arrived!

Ah, yes....Heroin, was sold by Bayer....And, yes, Bayer Aspirin, Bayer, who first aggressively advertised Heroin as the 'miracle treatment' for the Morphine hangover from the American Civil War. Yes, sir....Heroin was also touted as a Methadone-type opiate maintenance drug. Bayer promised that their snake oil Heroin would offer a painless release from Morphine. Sound familiar?

While working for a fabric dye factory in Germany, Friedrich Bayer & Company scientist, *Heinrich Dreser*, resurrected an old synthesis of morphine which had previously been chucked in the bad-idea-barrel by its original discoverer, Charles Romney Alder Wright. And after some experimentation on himself and some buddies around the fabric-dye shop, Dreser presented Heroin to the *Congress of German Naturalists and Physicians*. The following outtake written by *Cecil Munsey*—a great little piece, called, *HEROIN® and ASPIRIN® The Connection! & The Collection! - Part One*—best explains the fashion in which Dreser and Bayer misrepresented and aggressively marketed this medicine:

> In November eighteen-ninety-eight, Dreser presented the drug to the Congress of German Naturalists and Physicians, claiming it was ten times more effective as a cough medicine than codeine but had only a tenth of its toxic effects. It was also more effective than morphine as a painkiller. 'It was safe. It wasn't habit-forming.' In short, Dreser claimed it was a wonder drug.

So as it turns out, OxyContin seems to have learned their tricks from the masters, *who produced and marketed Opium Morphine and Heroin.*

As we all now know, Heroin quickly lost its medical luster as a 'Non-addictive Wonder Drug for the treatment of Morphine addiction' around a century ago, after mobs of Heroin addicts began stumbling around the East Coast like zombies. The so-called 'Junkie' Zombies collected junk metal to support their habits, hence the label, 'Junkie.' The public cried out for an end to the manmade plague. Heroin was then demonized by the medical industry and accepted by the US as the very cause of the epidemic, when Heroin was in fact Bayer's profitable 'non-addictive' solution for America's Morphine habit.

As another example of controlled conflict, Bayer offered an all-new painkiller-cure for the painful heroin vacuum: Aspirin. Aspirin, a relatively positive side to this mess, did little to ease withdrawal symptoms from heroin, but caught-on none-the-less. Aspirin—which also grows on trees—is a derivative of the bark of the willow tree known as *salicin*. Bayer now sells 29 billion tablets of Aspirin, every year.

In a merger of six companies, one of which being, Bayer, a new parent company, *IG Farben*, was formed on December nine, nineteen twenty-five, just in time for World War Two. IG Farben quickly began to employ slave labor at Farben's new work camp facility at Auschwitz, called, Buna Werke, since they became a huge government contractor for the Nazi takeover effort in Germany. Among IG Farben's government contracts in Germany, was the mass-production of Zyklon B, the poison gas which was released in large gas chambers disguised as showers during the holocaust.

IG Farben continued to operate after the Second World War, but in the early fifties this monster fanned back out, now cleverly camouflaged as its four original companies, which today, remain some of the world's largest pharmaceutical providers: Agfa, Sanofi, BASF—the largest chemical producer in the world—and, Bayer which as you know is enormous.

IG Farben was officially broken-up due to its affiliation with the Nazi regime. This seems very convenient since we can just point fingers at this now-defunct brand which produced gas for the gas chambers, after IG Farben's creepy little hatchlings quickly scattered into the world's industrial crevices. But where did these hatchlings scatter?

A video production on YouTube by James Corbett titled *Bayer + Monsanto = A Match Made in Hell* will take you from *'Devil Bill' Rockefeller's* cancer-snake-oil scam all the way through Standard oil and the four Nazi chemical companies it produced: Agfa, Sanofi, BASF, and Bayer. These four companies which came together to form the company which supplied the gas for the gas chambers (IG Farben) today supply all of our pharmaceutical companies. And now it seems they're again in the news in our times as they've overtaken the entire world's food supply.

This is where things get a little bit sketchy—okay, *a lot sketchy...Schering AG* was an international pharmaceutical company headquartered in Berlin. *Schering AG,* was bought by Bayer AG and merged to form the Bayer subsidiary, Bayer Schering Pharma AG, which was later renamed Bayer HealthCare Pharmaceuticals in 2011. Now for the good part: Enter, Arthur Sackler. In 1940, Arthur Sackler, founder of OxyContin maker, Purdue Pharma, became a pharmaceutical managing director, and head of the Medical Research Division, for this Nazi supply Company which developed and supplied the gas for Hitler's gas chambers disguised as *showers*.

Sacklers new conglomerate, *Schering Corporation* was established 'in preparation for its assignment of supplying and holding the foreign markets of Schering AG—the *company under the same corporate umbrella as Bayer who originally filed the trademark for the brand Heroin*—for the duration of the anticipated hostilities,' as Nazi Germany's wave of people-killing was coming to its final conclusion. So, essentially, Art Sackler was the US based Trustee for this Nazi supply company as they weathered the final firestorm when Nazi Germany was being toppled.

Two years later, Sackler's Schering Corporation was seized by the US government along with other companies having, 'German interests.' But following textbook Hegelian protocol, after the dust had all settled ten years later, the US government returned the four hundred forty-thousand shares of Schering stock which had been seized, and allowed the company to once again function independently. And though the confiscation of the company took place under Sackler's watch due to the companies collusion with the Nazis, Nazi brass must've determined that Art had done a stellar job, since his family was awarded the granddaddy of all opium Dynasties in America over a half century later: *OxyContin!*

This would probably be as good a time as any to mention that Prescott Bush, W's Granddad *who was initiated into the Order of Skull and Bones in nineteen-sixteen,* was also caught up in the same Nazi tentacles. In October nineteen forty-two, Union bank and Brown Brothers Harriman assets were seized under the Trading with the Enemy Act for financing the Nazi reign of terror; *Prescott Bush was the founding member and director of Brown Brothers Harriman and was also involved at a management level with Union Bank, at the time these assets were seized.*

Prescott Bush's father Samuel Bush also profited heavily from *his* involvement in the World Wars from his interest in steel manufacturing titan, *Buckeye Steel*. Without delving too far into the grimy details, Samuel Bush was also deeply mixed-up with the Harrimans, in the politics, armament and supply, and financing of both World Wars. The Harrimans are another Skull and Bones family of warmongers who've had their dirty hands in every American war since America's founding.

Aside from Heroin, Zyklon B nerve gas, *and,* the owner of the company who kicked off the OxyContin Dynasty, Bayer can also be linked to harboring high-level fugitive Nazi Germany war criminals, and assigning them powerful posts in these giant corporations after the toppling of the Hitler regime. NaturalNews.com posted an excellent article by Mike Adams *'the Health Ranger,'* from which I've extracted the following, eye-popping outtake:

Dr. Fritz ter Meer, a director of IG Farben who was directly involved in developing the nerve gas, Zyklon-B which killed millions, was sentenced to seven years in prison but was released after four years through the intervention of Rockefeller [a Skull and Bones family] and

J.J. McCloy, then US High Commissioner for Germany. An unrepentant Fritz ter Meer, guilty of genocide and crimes against humanity, returned to work in Bayer where he served as Chairman for more than ten years, until nineteen sixty-one.

The headline of this article written in May of two thousand sixteen, heralds:

'Nazi-founded Bayer chemical company wants to buy Satan-inspired Monsanto for forty-two billion... it's a perfect match made in chemical Hell'

And in the end Bayer *did* close on the deal with Monsanto just in time for the big news in August of two thousand eighteen. At which time a jury determined that Monsanto's weedkiller product 'Roundup' caused cancer in schoolchildren from contact with the poison. Roundup is used in most agricultural settings where food is grown for human consumption, and otherwise, still to this day. Now Bayer owns the agricultural weedkiller which a US Court has determined causes cancer in humans, *and* the patents on medicines with which they will treat you when you develop the malady.

Now, to summarize a shortlist of Bayer's collection of death-causing revenue-earning agents: This company brought us heroin, gas for the gas chambers, they invented leaded gasoline and have paid out millions in HIV infection cases due to AIDS-infected 'medicine' Bayer provided (which I'd explain but I don't want to lose continuity), and they now own Monsanto which a court in the US determines 'causes cancer.' *Oh*, and it appears that the gentleman who brought us the OxyContin genocide *and drug advertising in America* was also mixed up with these Nazi creeps. But never fear, just like Bayer's dirty past, time will wash this company clean of its sins in preparation for its nexus for who knows what kind of dirty deeds.

Bayer, Monsanto's new owner, is now changing the name of Monsanto, just as the Nazi company IG Farben did to insulate Bayer for the years during and right after the Second World War. Monsanto will now distribute their products, fittingly, under the name, 'Bayer.'

And in a related newsworthy matter… Yale recently purchased the *Bayer Medical Campus* and *Labs* which was already virtually located on the campus of Yale University.

10. Methadone - Opium Dynasty Four

After the Second World War, the number of Junkies addicted to America's miracle addiction drug, Heroin, had again spiraled out of control. The East Coast was once more flooded with 'Junk'-metal-Zombies. In New York City, the average age of death came to the Heroin user at the tender age of twenty-nine.

Along with our war plunder came a recipe for a drug called Methadone which was born in a German lab in nineteen thirty-nine. Methadone's popularity as a painkiller grew some, but was never broadly accepted due to its side-effects: Methadone was found to cause extreme Nausea and exhibited a high instance of overdose; plainly speaking, even Hitler wouldn't use this poison on his own people. Despite these known dangers, America adopted Germany's reject opiate as the cure to Heroin addiction, which spawned the Methadone clinics of Methadone's Opium Dynasty.

11. Oxycontin - Opium Dynasty Five

As we've learned, OxyContin was a black-Nazi-horse which we've simply stopped beating, helped back to his hooves, and then boosted its rider back onto the beast and simply allowed it to 'ride off into the sunset' to find new markets throughout the world.

12. Suboxone - Opium Dynasty Six

Near the end of his final term, the Evil Empire's apparent spokesperson, Barack Obama, participated in a televised charade in which he again demonized the old miracle cure for opium addiction, OxyContin, and in which he ushers in Washington, Pharma, and Wall Street's next synthetic Opium Dynasty, Buprenorphine, the active ingredient in Suboxone, the new miracle opiate medicine.

I have seen for myself that Buprenorphine is the most vile and addictive synthetic opium that technology has ever conceived and America is again poising to shove this synthetic opium down our throats as, 'The New Miracle Cure For Addiction,' just as they have time-and-time-before. Remember, in order to make Suboxone, one would require beautiful fields of opium poppies which grow right next to the same pretty flowers with which one would produce heroin and Oxycontin.

Reckitt Benckiser, the firm who was awarded the golden-ticket-miracle-drug Suboxone, had its share of overdose deaths itself—many. And what's more disturbing, is the fact that they've been sued for multiple incidents involving dead babies, which shouldn't be terribly surprising since nearly all of their products are the traditional forms of baby prevention and poison—*condoms and household cleaners.* In fact, Reckitt Benckiser has been proven responsible for deaths from multiple products, including a South Korean debacle which involved more than ninety deaths linked to disinfectants. The company's OTC painkiller Nurofen has also been linked to many deaths.

Despite all of these and countless other legal hiccups associated with this company which is worthy of its own documentary, their CEO has been one of the highest paid in the world, raking-in a whopping twenty-three point two million Pounds Sterling in two thousand fifteen—which if you're counting, is over thirty-million American Dollars in a single year.

Believe it or not, the CEO who rakes in all of this cash for the new Suboxone Opium Dynasty is none other than an Eastern Indian gentleman who shares his last name with the man who meddled in Arizona's over-the-counter marijuana measure, sparking the research which began this whole adventure. The name of **British**-owned Reckitt Benckiser's key man is Raresh **Kapoor**. Both Mr. Kapoors specialize in sublingual opiate diseases and cures. And perhaps it's by no coincidence that these cohorts sharing the same surname were both awarded high-level 'golden-ticket'-posts within the evil empire from which to inch this lumbering beast forward. Both Mr. Kapoors can be linked back to the Sassoon family who are also known as the *Rothschilds of the East*.

The Sassoon family were **a Royal Eastern-Indian dope-dealing cabal who historically worked closely with the British East India Company which converted the whole country of India into a gulag**, whose sole function was the production of opium which was then spread around the world. For a world of discovery, the families and dirty deeds of The Order of Skull and Bones on Yale University *and their connection to the dope-dealing British East India Company* can be further explored in my Bestselling Amazon Series, *Sacred Scroll of Seven Seals.*

Obama and his cronies recently blew the air horn which kicked-off the Suboxone boom after the patent for Suboxone expired, which, I am sure is why Mr. Kapoor took the giant pay cut which has been heralded from every money-news source on the planet. In the video link provided below, after a well-placed Suboxone testimonial, Sanjay Gupta and President Obama admit exactly how they ushered in the OxyContin Dynasty. Which is nearly word-for-word how the video began when they were pitching Suboxone. You really should watch the entire video, (YouTube: 'Obama turns attention to growing opioid abuse problem': https://www.youtube.com/watch?v=Lt_2uXRVMNA) but at minimum you should scrub it to 19:58…And if you didn't have time to listen to the video at all, Obama states:

'...this is a shift, that began very early on in my administration. And, you know...there's a reason, why, uh...my drug czar, uh...is somebody who came not from the criminal justice side but came really from the treatment side and himself has been in recovery for decades now, because, it's...this is something that I think we understood fairly early on...now, uh...I'm gonna be blunt, I hope you don't mind. I was saying in a speech yesterday: Your last year in office you just get a little loose...'

In the video, Obama even throws another Billion dollars of your hard-earned money at the misinformation outlets of this country, in order to push this boon into its intended pockets. And with his most-generous endowment to this invented 'crisis,' I hope that Obama has made it perfectly 'clear' to you that Hitler's done a little remodeling over the years...but his gulags always slowly evolve into the same old place.

If you get time, scrub the video to 48:11, at which point, Obama, Gupta, and their dupe-professional, will explain, in their own words, exactly how they kicked-off the OxyContin

Dynasty of opiates! Which strongly resembles the way this cringe-worthy video began when they were pitching their Suboxone dope-game. You really should watch the whole painful episode but if you don't have the stomach for it, you already have the general idea...

This shift has pushed America's new wave of addicts into the only treatment games offered by this country: *Heroin*, other street drugs like *'gray death' Fentanyl*, or an even-stronger synthetic dope like Obama's new 'opioid'-based solution to opiate addiction: *Suboxone!* Which is the hardest opiate in the world from which to physically withdraw! That is the real value of this patent.

And this tale of 'two, old haggard witches' who've constantly washed us 'clean' with 'muddy water,' *back-and-forth,* has been repeated time-and-time again throughout America's history, due solely to misinformation. Hopefully, one day we will tire of these two old and deceptive 'hags' and put them to rest once and for all. Invariably, I maintain that one should reserve the right to use Suboxone to treat opiate addiction, if one chooses to do so after being warned.

It is probably fairly evident to even the casual onlooker now, that, if the US Government was truly worried about the citizens of this country, they would most likely just give back all of the plants which contained our natural medicines in the first place, and turn the pharmaceutical clock back to just before the Civil War, a time in America when there was no such thing as the 'disease' of addiction—the cause of which was identified by twelve brave Congress-People to be: *Greed!*

I'm sure that you're somewhat disappointed that we didn't have the time to dig a little deeper into the substance which saved my life but if you look at the title of this work, it doesn't exactly imply anything about a cure. I didn't want to lose folks with all of that psychedelic talk before the, 'roundup,' of all of these bad-guys was complete; so perhaps this will give us something to look forward to in the future...but I did leave you with the name of the gift which you should heavily research on your own anyway if considering.

13. 'If it Weren't for You Meddling Kids...'

...Well, I guess that the end of any *'epic tale of conspiracy, murder, genocide, and greed,'* should offer a tidy wrap-up of its characters, even if those roughed-up and disheveled, unmasked 'villains,' *are* 'bad actors'...

Arthur Sackler died in the decade before the culmination of his many talents (psychiatry, advertising, and that of being a medical doctor) would reap the payoff which became the OxyContin Dynasty. With Arthur's head start, his two brothers, Raymond and Mortimer, went on to usher-in the OxyContin wave of opium well into this century and they've left behind a bucket-load of misery and a legacy of evil which will leave those who follow in their footsteps hard pressed to outshine; but I am sure that their ilk have some amazing magic tricks up their sleeves.

Mortimer David Sackler died March twenty-four, two thousand ten. And Raymond Sackler followed him in death on July seventeen, two thousand seventeen. The Sackler family remains one of the richest in the world, among whom, key men have been appointed to throw money at new endeavors.

Every time I see photos of these guys, I crack up because they remind me of the rich dudes on that Richard Pryor movie, *Trading Places*.

As for Insys founder and Arizona voter-manipulator, *John Kapoor*—who single-handedly snuffed the proposition for safe, over-the-counter pain relief in the state of Arizona—we will use another outtake from Forbes.com to dramatize his fate:

'John Kapoor, billionaire founder of opioid spray manufacturer Insys Therapeutics, was arrested in Phoenix on Thursday morning and charged with RICO conspiracy, conspiracy to commit mail and wire fraud, and conspiracy to violate the Anti-Kickback law. Forbes reached out to Insys on Thursday morning but has not heard back yet. An attorney for Kapoor told CBS News, that Kapoor, 'is innocent of these charges and intends to fight the charges vigorously....'

And even though the courts again overlooked the one charge, *serial murder*, John currently fights the balance of these organized criminal charges from his jail cell. Wait. Before you get all choked up, it's only four years in one of those cushy joints and he still sells his deadly breath-spray from behind bars. *And unfortunately*, I'm sure there's a crowd just like him bunched up in his shadows, waiting their turn for a ride on the back of this many-headed hydra.

And for those without souls, why wouldn't they? After all, Kapoor too recently joined the Sackler Oxycontin Dynasty Family on the Forbes list of richest people in the world, ranked at 335th with a net worth of a *whopping* two point one Billion dollars! In the Forbes article below, Kapoor explains precisely how he murdered his victims in exchange for his fortune, as he describes the intellectual value of his worthless patent:

'Even though we were the number five to come into the market, the big advantage of our product [Fentanyl] is it's active in three to five minutes,' ...

But as stated, Fentanyl, one of the strongest opiates ever offered, should **not** be offered in a rapid-delivery-'packaging' and sent home for self-administration. This is reminiscent of the older 'packaging' patents in which opiates were offered: Syringes loaded with Morphine and 'Atomic Percocet!' Which have been killing people in the very same way since time began: TOO MUCH DOPE TOO FAST....***Pow!*** *And yes*, syringes *are* 'good'... but technology is a double-edged sword and as long as there's a buck to be made, a body will generally lie on the ground. It's not rocket science...

I know that there will be a lot of scrutiny of this piece by the medical industry; I understand their frustration and I anticipate the wave of violent comments and one-star-reviews which are sure to follow this publication....I get it, no one wants to hear that most of what they've been taught concerning *history* as well as an entire swath of their field is all lies, or that your profession has been killing people for profit for centuries. I understand why this would make practitioners in the field uncomfortable. Most of these caretakers have tender hearts and were even inspired to work in their field by their own journeys down this dark and lonely path.

But just as I learned in Narcotics Anonymous 'in the little time I was there,' we have to understand that what we're doing is wrong—by, 'admitting' that we 'have a problem' before we can rehabilitate the entire educational, medical and governmental systems. We can no-longer allow our children to be led to heroin and illicit pharmaceuticals with misinformation and 'atomic' doses of mislabeled drugs which are delivered too fast, after which our kids are demonized and then just tossed in the fire once they've become toxic to their 'healthcare providers' from the final stages of this affliction.

It was misinformation which led souls to death camps like Auschwitz, from mislabeled cattle-cars to gas chambers labeled as 'showers'—which is precisely the *same mechanism with which we are being dispatched in America today: deception and murder for profit.* It is just concealed in a far more clever 'packaging' since technology has now painted the patient as *defective* and therefore *disposable.* This is the true purpose for the technology of 'Survival of the Fittest'—aka *Darwinism.* And it is precisely the same trust of sinister minds who continue to ride this beast through time for profit.

In exchange for a small cut of the profits, *Every* government will *always* simply line the pockets of people like the privileged bloodliners of the *British East India Company* who spread dope to the entire world during and after the Opium Wars, the Russells who dealt Morphine during and after the Civil War in America, Bayer who invented heroin as the cure to our leftover morphine addiction from the Civil War, the Sacklers who 'packaged' 'atomic Percocet' at Purdue Pharma, and bad actors like John Kapoor at Insys, until we demand change and stop allowing our children to be thrown wholesale into this fire, which is being fed by the prevailing winds of misinformation as we speak.

Purdue Pharma has now set a new legal and medical precedent which legitimizes doctors as little more than dope-dealers if they so-choose to be. This has left nothing more than a doctor's paper-thin sheet of moral fabric stretched hopelessly between his patient's life and the red hot belly of this furnace, rather than just offering citizens factual information and a set of ground rules by which to safely ingest a substance, if patients still choose to do-so after being warned.

No matter how we choose to proceed from here, this problem won't be fixed overnight, if at all. But we *can* educate others and do those little things throughout each day which *could* slowly build a social model which *could* result in us 'shifting' our minds and hearts, laws, curriculums and governmental agencies rather than just 'shifting' to higher doses of stronger dope which is even tougher to 'kick.'

Written in Memory of a loving father of three and drug war casualty, my Big Brother: 'Joey!'

Thanks for listening,

Judah

'Nothing so needs reforming as other people's habits. Fanatics will never learn that, though it be written in letters of gold across the sky. It is the prohibition that makes anything precious.'

- Mark Twain -

Collaboration Opportunity

This paper began as a script for a documentary film. And though I'd already had the funds and crew in place to shoot this film, I did NOT wish to lose control of this information, which was part of the deal. Despite this lucrative contract, it is far more important, to me, that this information make its way to Americans, unmolested. If you would like to join me in a thankless effort to turn these policies around before they blossom into a mess which will make Nazi Germany look like a petting zoo, please contact me to discuss a partnership which will make this information available to Americans everywhere. 'Judah' :

JudahVisionMail@Gmail.com

Please go to Amazon.com to let Judah know how he did on his New Release: Hitler's New Shower!

And if you haven't yet, read Sacred Scroll of Seven Seals to pick up where this book left off—the families of the Order of Skull & Bones on Yale University, and their history of wrongdoing!

Another great course of discovery, Book II of the Sacred Scroll of Seven Seals Series, 'Back Upright,' connects the bloodlines and rituals of the Order of Skull and Bones back to the Bible.

Also, please make the time to visit and subscribe-to Judah's new YouTube Channel, Judah Vision, covering topics which range from analyzing predictive programming in pop culture to the identification and study of the rituals of Freemasonry.

CPSIA information can be obtained
at www.ICGtesting.com
Printed in the USA
FSHW01n0616051018
52776FS